WILDLIFE WORLDS

AUSTRALIA
ANDANTARCTICA

TIM HARRIS

CRABTREE
PUBLISHING COMPANY
WWW.CRABTREEBOOKS.COM

CRABTREE
PUBLISHING COMPANY
WWW.CRABTREEBOOKS.COM

Published in Canada
Crabtree Publishing
616 Welland Avenue
St. Catharines, ON
L2M 5V6

Published in the United States
Crabtree Publishing
PMB 59051
350 Fifth Ave, 59th Floor
New York, NY 10118

Published in 2020 by Crabtree Publishing Company

First published in Great Britain in 2019 by The Watts Publishing Group
Copyright © The Watts Publishing Group 2019

Printed in the U.S.A./122019/CG20191101

With thanks to the Nature Picture Library

Author: Tim Harris

Editorial director: Kathy Middleton

Editors: Amy Pimperton, Robin Johnson

Series Designer: Nic Davies smartdesignstudio.co.uk

Photo researchers: Rachelle Morris (Nature Picture Library), Laura Sutherland (Nature Picture Library), Diana Morris

Proofreader: Wendy Scavuzzo

Production coordinator and prepress: Tammy McGarr

Print coordinator: Katherine Berti

Photo credits:
Dreamstime: Carol Buchanan 3b, 9tl; Awcnz62 5b.
FLPA Images: Michael & Patricia Fogden/Minden Pictures 21c.
Nature PL: Georgette Douwma 9tr; Jurgen Freund 9c, 10-11, 12-13c, 13tl, 14c, 17c; Tim Laman 18-19,19tr, 19cr, 19br; Jiri Lochman 6br, 15bl; Steven David Miller 6c; Fred Oliver 29b; Inaki Relanzon 2b, 8c; Richard Robinson 25tr; Tui De Roi 21tl, 23br; Brent Stephenson 24r; Paul D Stewart 18bl; Andy Trowbridge 22-23; Robert Valentic 17br; Visuals Unlimited 7t; Dave Watts 6bl; Doc White 27br.
Shutterstock: Marcos Amend 29tr; Anneka 7br; Ingo Arndt 27bl; Kristian Bell 17t; Blue Planet Studio 23tr, 24bl; BMJ front cover b; Willyam Bradberry back cover tr, 3c, 25b; John Carnemolla 4cl, 11b; Joshua Daniel back cover tcl, 21tr; Feathercollector 19bc; Dale Lorna Jacobsen 29tl. Shaun Jeffers 2t, 20; Peter Leahy 7bl; Nounours 15c; Bruno Paganelli 28; Pierdest 14bl, 31cr; Daniel Poloha 25tl; Tim Pryce back cover tl, 16c, 32t; Cheryl Ramalho 26-27c; redcarpet19 6t; Reptiles4all 23cr; Marina Riley front cover c; Phillip Schubert 16bl, 17bl, 30br; Luke Shelley 11tl, 13br, 30tr, 32; Sirtravelalot back cover tc, 3t, 27tl; Szefei 5t;Tarpan 27r; Vladsilver 4b; Vojce 8b; Andrew Walmsley 11tr; Yatra front cover t, 4cr; Bildagenteur Zoonar GmbH: 1, 13tr.
Wikimedia Commons: Christopher Watson/CC-BY-SA 3.0 11tcr.

Library and Archives Canada Cataloguing in Publication

Title: Australia and Antarctica / Tim Harris.
Other titles: Australasia and Antarctica
Names: Harris, Tim (Ornithologist), author.
Description: Series statement: Wildlife worlds |
  Previously published under title: Australasia and Antarctica. London:
  Franklin Watts, 2019. | Includes index.
Identifiers: Canadiana (print) 20190200626 |
  Canadiana (ebook) 20190200642 |
  ISBN 9780778776796 (hardcover) | ISBN 9780778776857 (softcover) |
  ISBN 9781427125330 (HTML)
Subjects: LCSH: Animals—Australia—Juvenile literature. | LCSH:
  Animals—Antarctica—Juvenile literature. | LCSH: Habitat (Ecology)—
  Australia—Juvenile literature. | LCSH: Habitat (Ecology)—Antarctica—
  Juvenile literature. | LCSH: Natural history—Australia—Juvenile
  literature. | LCSH: Natural history—Antarctica—Juvenile literature.
  | LCSH: Australia—Juvenile literature. | LCSH: Antarctica—Juvenile
  literature.
Classification: LCC QL338 .H37 2020 | DDC j591.99—dc23

Library of Congress Cataloging-in-Publication Data

Names: Harris, Tim (Ornithologist), author.
Title: Australia and Antarctica / Tim Harris.
Description: New York : Crabtree Publishing Company, 2020. |
  Series: Wildlife worlds | Includes index.
Identifiers: LCCN 2019043587 (print) | LCCN 2019043588 (ebook) |
  ISBN 9780778776796 (hardcover) |
  ISBN 9780778776857 (paperback) |
  ISBN 9781427125330 (ebook)
Subjects: LCSH: Animals--Australia--Juvenile literature. | Plants--
  Australia--Juvenile literature. | Animals--Antarctica--Juvenile literature.
  | Plants--Antarctica--Juvenile literature.
Classification: LCC QL338 .H37 2020 (print) | LCC QL338 (ebook) |
  DDC 591.994--dc23
LC record available at https://lccn.loc.gov/2019043587
LC ebook record available at https://lccn.loc.gov/2019043588

Contents

Australia and Antarctica

Australia is the smallest continent on Earth. The continent is made up of the island of Australia, as well as the islands of New Zealand, New Guinea, and thousands of smaller islands in the Pacific Ocean. Antarctica is the continent that is farthest south. Although it is almost twice the size of Australia, hardly anyone lives there because it is a bitterly cold, ice-covered **desert**. It is also the driest and windiest continent.

Australia is surrounded by the Pacific, Southern, and Indian Oceans. Much of the continent receives very little rainfall, and is either desert or dry **scrubland** and grassland. There are, however, **tropical rain forests** in the northeast and **temperate** forests in the Great Barrier Range in the southeast. Running along the east coast is the Great Barrier **Reef**. The reef and forests are home to a wide variety of plants and animals, many of which are found nowhere else on Earth.

KANGAROO   KOALA

Kangaroos and koalas are **marsupials native** to Australia.

EMPEROR PENGUIN

4

Much of New Guinea is covered by rain forest. Birds of paradise and many other amazing wildlife live on this tropical island.

New Guinea

Foja Mountains

GREATER BIRD OF PARADISE

Indian Ocean

Daintree Rain Forest

Karijini National Park

Bungle Bungles

Great Barrier Reef

Pacific Ocean

Uluru (Ayers Rock)

New Zealand's two islands have high mountains, **glaclers**, and rocky coastlines. Albatross, flightless kiwis, and other interesting birds live there.

Australia

Lake Eyre

Penguins and other seabirds live around Antarctica's coast. No animals or plants can survive in the continent's frozen **interior**.

Southern Ocean

Tasmania

Waipoua Forest

Southern Alps

North Island

Fiordland

New Zealand

South Island

Weddell Sea

Antarctica

Ross Ice Shelf

Ross Island

KIWI

Daintree Rain Forest

Daintree is Australia's largest and oldest tropical rain forest. It has grown there for more than 135 million years. The forest is home to a greater variety of animals and plants than any other place in this massive country.

Boardwalks and trails help visitors explore this beautiful national park, which lies on the coast of the Pacific Ocean. There are unspoiled beaches, and rock peaks that tower over the kauri pines and other trees. There are also some very heavy downpours in this rain forest!

Buff-breasted paradise kingfishers swoop down from trees in the rain forest to catch tasty insects or frogs on the ground below.

A large, prickly insect called a katydid is well hidden on the trunk of a tree.

The Daintree Rain Forest has some very unusual animals. Sugar gliders (below) are marsupials that glide through the air from tree to tree. Platypuses are strange-looking, egg-laying mammals with beaks like ducks. Large flightless birds called cassowaries (left) are sometimes seen in the forest.

The wings of a Cairns birdwing butterfly sparkle in the sunlight.

White-lipped tree frogs can grow to 5.5 inches (14 cm) long.

Great Barrier Reef

The Great Barrier Reef stretches more than 1,430 miles (2,300 km) in the warm, shallow waters off the coast of northeastern Australia. It is the world's largest reef system.

The Great Barrier Reef provides shelter and food for millions of fish, crabs, lobsters, **mollusks**, and other **aquatic** animals. Tiny **plankton** drift in the warm waters around the reef. Large animals such as sea turtles, dolphins, and whales visit the reef to feed.

The reef has been built up by animals called coral polyps over many thousands of years. These animals attach themselves to underwater rocks and divide to form a **colony**. Some corals are stony and some are soft. When a stony coral dies, its hard **limestone** skeleton remains, adding a little to the size of the reef.

Colorful clownfish often live with stinging animals called sea anemones that protect them from **predators**.

Giant clams can live for 100 years or more. They settle in one place on the reef and stay there for the rest of their lives.

Adult sea turtles visit the reef to feed on sea grasses and **algae**.

Uluru

Rising high above the hot, dry Australian **outback** is a rock so huge that it takes more than three hours to walk around it. Uluru, or Ayers Rock, is made of ancient **sandstone** that glows orange and red at sunrise and sunset. It is a **sacred** site for the Anangu **Aboriginal** people.

Uluru dominates the countryside for miles around. The giant rock towers 1,142 feet (348 m) above the surrounding desert, making it taller than the Statue of Liberty in New York. Most of the animals that live near Uluru shelter from the Sun's heat during the day. Bats sleep in rock **crevices**, while lizards and other small animals stay cool in their **burrows**.

Wedge-tailed eagles (left) soar above Uluru, hunting lizards and other small **prey**. Down below, wild dogs called dingoes hunt in the desert and dazzling fairywrens (right) perch on bushes.

Barking spiders live in burrows in the desert. They rub parts of their mouths together to make a barking sound to scare off predators.

Red kangaroos are large animals with long tails. They can hop much faster than humans can run, and can cover 25 feet (7.6 m) in a single leap.

Lake Eyre

Any rain that falls on a vast area of the Australian outback collects in a large drainage basin. This area, which covers one-sixth of the country, is called the Lake Eyre Basin. Unlike most drainage basins, its major rivers do not flow to the sea. Instead the water flows slowly toward the shallow and salty Lake Eyre.

The Lake Eyre Basin is hot and very dry most of the time. The water flowing in the rivers **evaporates** before it gets to the lake, which remains bone-dry. Once in a while, though, very heavy rainfall fills the rivers and Lake Eyre floods. Then many thousands of pelicans, terns, stilts, and other waterbirds fly there to feed and raise their young.

Lake Eyre has not been completely full of water since 1974. Even then, it was only 20 feet (6 m) deep. The pink color of the lake is caused by tiny algae that thrive in salty water.

Dusky hopping mice live in burrows more than 3 feet (1 m) deep. They get all the water they need from their food.

The sharp spines of a thorny devil warn predators not to attack.

When Lake Eyre fills with water, red-necked avocets and other birds visit to feed.

Bungle Bungles

Hundreds of rock towers rise from the flat land of the Tanami Desert in Western Australia. The rocks, called the Bungle Bungles, are shaped like beehives. A closer look reveals that there are orange and gray stripes across the rocks.

The Bungle Bungles were formed when sand and small pieces of rock were carried by rivers to the bottom of an ocean millions of years ago. The sand and rocks were pressed together and, over time, hardened into tough rock called sandstone. Then, movements of Earth's **crust** raised the sandstone to where it sits now.

Occasional heavy rainfall and the action of the wind have carved the rocks into their unusual shapes. The rain and wind have also cut **gorges** into the sandstone in some places.

Gouldian finches are some of the most colorful birds in the world, and can sometimes be spotted in the Bungle Bungles. They eat mostly grass seeds.

Green birdflowers grow in the sandy areas around the Bungle Bungle rocks. The flowers look like birds hanging on to the plant's stem with their beaks.

Karijini National Park

Karijini National Park is a very dry part of Western Australia. It is the traditional home of the Banyjima, Kurrama, and Innawonga peoples, who have lived there for at least 20,000 years.

Rivers and waterfalls have **eroded** beautiful gorges into ancient red and orange rocks. It is often baking hot there during the summer, and thunderstorms bring heavy rains that fill deep pools. Many of the animals that live there only become active at night, when it is cooler.

A female spiny echidna lays a single egg. The baby, called a puggle, hatches, then grows in its mother's **pouch** for two or three months.

Rabbit-sized bilbies have long ears and tails. They are active at night and shelter in burrows during the heat of the day.

In the cooler months, the land is covered with yellow-flowering trees called cassias and wattles, and purple shrubs called mulla-mullas (left).

Desert death adders live in Karijini National Park. They grow to only 28 inches (70 cm) but are some of the most **venomous** snakes on Earth.

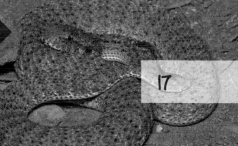

Foja Mountains

On the giant tropical island of New Guinea lie the Foja Mountains, one of the most **remote** areas on Earth. No roads pass through these mountains, and only a very few people live there.

The mountains are covered in rainforest trees, which are often draped in clouds. Rain can fall at any time, but it is heaviest from December to March. Several recent **expeditions** have discovered animals that were not known before or had not been seen for many years, including species of frogs, butterflies, birds, and mammals.

The **dense** forests are home to an amazing variety of animals. Male birds of paradise perform wild mating dances on tree branches, while male bowerbirds (left) build shelters made of twigs to attract females. Snakes lie in wait to attack their prey.

Pinocchio frogs were first discovered in the Foja Mountains in 2008. Males can make their noses stick out with air when they call.

Long-tailed pygmy possums are excellent climbers. They use their **prehensile** tails to hold on to branches.

Tiny blossom bats feed on flowers. They are only 2 inches (6 cm) long.

LESSER BIRD OF PARADISE

Waipoua Forest

The Waipoua Forest lies in the warm northern part of New Zealand's North Island, close to the Kauri Coast. It contains many ancient kauri trees, which are some of the oldest trees on Earth. These giant **conifers** tower above all the other trees in the forest.

The native Maori people considered the kauris to be the kings of the forest. European settlers later used wood from the trees to make ships. Now, the forest is protected and is home to birds, amphibians, and a rich variety of orchids and other plants.

The Maori people call the largest kauri tree "Tāne Mahuta," or Lord of the Forest. It is 148 feet (45 m) tall, and is believed to be at least 2,300 years old.

The flightless North Island brown kiwi searches fallen leaves for earthworms and beetle larvae.

Red-crowned parakeets eat fruit, flowers, seeds, and buds.

Archey's frogs are native to the North Island of New Zealand and are not found anywhere else on Earth.

Southern Alps

The Southern Alps form a mighty range of mountains on New Zealand's South Island. There are many steep-sided peaks and Aoraki, or Mount Cook, is the biggest of them all. The highest slopes of the mountains are covered in ice and snow even in the summer.

AORAKI

Winds blowing from the ocean bring heavy rain or snow to the western slopes. Fast-flowing streams and rivers carry the rain to the sea. Over thousands of years, the snow has turned to ice and formed dozens of glaciers high in the mountains. On the lower slopes, **lush** rain forests grow.

Aoraki rises 12,218 feet (3,724 m) above sea level and is New Zealand's highest mountain, but it was once even higher. In 1991, millions of tons of rock came crashing down from the **summit**, losing 98 feet (30 m) of its height.

Lupins flower near Lake Tekapo every summer. The lake is in a valley that was cut by glacial ice thousands of years ago.

The Southern Alps gecko lives among the rocks, **scree**, and scrubland on the mountains.

The kea is the world's only **alpine** parrot. It nests in burrows under tree roots and can survive the harsh mountain winters.

23

Fiordland

Fiordland is a region in the far southwestern corner of New Zealand's South Island. It contains a series of deep, narrow **inlets** of the sea called **fiords** that were carved by glaciers thousands of years ago.

As rainfall drains through the lush forests on the slopes above the fiords, it becomes stained brown by the rotting leaves on the ground. This dark, fresh water does not mix with the seawater in the fiords, but sits on top of it instead. This limits the amount of sunlight that reaches the depths of the fiords and keeps most of the marine life in the top 131 feet (40 m) of water.

Stirling Falls (above right) plunges 492 feet (150 m) down cliffs and into a fiord called Milford Sound. The falls create spray that inspired its Maori name "cloud on the water." A large mountain called Mitre Peak (above left) towers over the fiord.

Some blue cod are so tame that they swim up to divers in the fiords.

Fiordland crested penguins breed among tree roots and rocks close to the coast, where they can easily dive into the sea.

Bottlenose dolphins swim together in groups called pods that often contain 10 to 15 animals. They visit the New Zealand fiords in search of fish to eat.

Weddell Sea

The Weddell Sea is a very large bite-shaped inlet in the coastline of western Antarctica. Billions of tiny animals called krill live in its waters. They provide food for thousands of seals and penguins, as well as hundreds of whales.

On one side of the Weddell Sea, the long, thin Antarctic **Peninsula** reaches hundreds of miles into the Southern Ocean. The mountainous peninsula has big colonies of breeding seals, penguins, gulls, and other seabirds. Although the weather there is freezing cold, it is not as bitter as in the rest of Antarctica.

Much of the Weddell Sea is covered by an **ice shelf** up to 1,970 feet (600 m) thick. Deep cracks called crevasses run through this ice.

The pure-white snow petrel feeds on krill, fish, and squid that it catches from the ocean surface or just below it.

Antarctic krill grow to just 2 inches (6 cm) long. Without these small **crustaceans**, many animals would starve.

The blue whale is the world's largest animal. It visits the deep waters of the Weddell Sea to feed on krill.

27

Ross Island and the Ross Ice Shelf

Ross Island is an island near Antarctica formed by four volcanoes. Earth's southernmost active volcano, Mount Erebus, is located on Ross Island. Its summit is nearly 12,448 feet (3,794 m) above sea level. There, temperatures fall to -58 degrees Fahrenheit (-50 °C) and very strong winds are common, making it too cold for animals to survive.

Ice from Antarctica's interior slowly moves to the coast and spreads over the ocean to form the Ross Ice Shelf off the coast of Ross Island. Seals, penguins, and seabirds live around the edge of the ice shelf. Whales and dolphins swim offshore, and albatross glide on the strong winds that blow over the Southern Ocean.

The Ross Ice Shelf is the largest body of floating ice in the world. Huge **icebergs** often calve, or break off, from it and float out to sea.

Leopard seals are clumsy on ice, but they swim quickly in water. These large seals hunt penguins and smaller seals.

Emperor penguins travel long distances across the ice to breed in colonies each year. The female lays one egg, then returns to the ocean to feed. The male (above) **incubates** the egg until it hatches two months later.

Glossary

Aboriginal Living in an area before colonists arrived

algae Very small plant-like life-forms

alpine Relating to high mountains

aquatic Living in water

burrow A hole or tunnel in the ground that an animal makes to live in or for safety

colony A group of one kind of animal living close together

conifer An evergreen tree that produces cones

crevice A crack in rock

crust The outer layer of Earth

crustacean A kind of animal, such as a lobster or crab, that has an external skeleton but no backbone

dense Growing close together

desert A place that receives little or no rainfall and has few or no plants

eroded Worn away by the action of rain, waves, or wind

evaporate To change from a liquid to a gas

expedition A journey taken by a group of people for scientific research or other purposes

fiord A narrow sea inlet between cliffs or steep slopes

glacier A large body of ice moving slowly down a valley

gorge A narrow valley with steep-sided walls and usually a stream at the bottom

ice shelf A floating sheet of ice that is permanently attached to land

iceberg A large mass of ice that has broken off a glacier and is floating in the ocean

incubate To sit on an egg to keep it warm before it hatches

inlet A narrow area of water that goes into the land from a sea or lake

interior The part of a country or continent that is far from the coast

limestone Rock formed from fossilized animal skeletons and shells

lush Growing thick and healthy

marsupial A mammal that carries its young in a pocket of skin on the mother's stomach

mollusk A soft-bodied animal, such as a slug or clam, that has no backbone

native Living or growing naturally in an area

outback A vast inland area of Australia that is far away from places most people live

peninsula A piece of land that is almost totally surrounded by water, but is not quite an island

plankton Tiny animal and plant life that floats in water

pouch A pocket of skin on some female animals that is used to carry young

predators Animals that kill and eat other animals

prehensile Able to grab or to wrap around branches

prey Animals that are killed and eaten by other animals

rain forest A dense forest that receives a high amount of rainfall

reef A ridge of coral, rock, or sand that lies just above or below the ocean's surface

remote Far away from where most people live

sacred Of religious or spiritual importance

sandstone Rock made of grains of sand or quartz that have been pressed together over time

scree Loose stones that cover a slope

scrubland A dry area that has small, poorly grown shrubs or trees

summit The very top

temperate Describing forests found in moderate climates

tropical Relating to the tropics, the areas above and below the equator

venomous Producing chemicals that can injure or kill prey

Further Information

Books

Friedman, Mel. *Australia and Oceania*. Scholastic, 2009.

Hyde, Natalie. *Great Barrier Reef Research Journal*. Crabtree Publishing, 2018.

Kellaher, Karen. *Antarctica*. Scholastic, 2019.

Rockett, Paul. *Mapping Australia and Oceania, and Antarctica*. Crabtree Publishing, 2017.

Websites

www.kids.nationalgeographic.com/videos/destination-world/#/1252876867883
Fun facts about the frozen continent of Antarctica.

www.ducksters.com/geography/oceania.php
This website has profiles of Australia, New Zealand, Papua New Guinea, and other island countries.

www.barrierreef.org/
Visit this website for creature features and facts about the reef.

www.nationalgeographic.com/animals/index/
Type in the names of animals and get lots of fascinating facts about mammals, reptiles, amphibians, fish, and birds.

Index